P9-CSB-973

SCIENCE MADE SIMPLE™

ELECTRIC AND MAGNETIC PHENOMENA

DEAN GALIANO

Property of Library
Cape Fear Community College
Wilmington, NC 28401-3910

rosen publishing's
rosen central®

New York

Published in 2011 by The Rosen Publishing Group, Inc.
29 East 21st Street, New York, NY 10010

Copyright © 2011 by The Rosen Publishing Group, Inc.

First Edition

All rights reserved. No part of this book may be reproduced in any form without permission in writing from the publisher, except by a reviewer.

Library of Congress Cataloging-in-Publication Data

Galiano, Dean.
Electric and magnetic phenomena / Dean Galiano. — 1st ed.
    p. cm. — (Science made simple)
Includes bibliographical references and index.
ISBN 978-1-4488-1231-8 (lib. bdg.)
ISBN 978-1-4488-2239-3 (pbk.)
ISBN 978-1-4488-2247-8 (6-pack)
1. Electricity—Juvenile literature. 2. Magnetism—Juvenile literature. I. Title.
QC527.2.G35 2011
537—dc22

2010014546

Manufactured in Malaysia

CPSIA Compliance Information: Batch #W11YA: For further information, contact Rosen Publishing, New York, New York, at 1-800-237-9932.

On the cover: Top: This photo shows the aurora borealis, or northern lights, as seen over Fairbanks, Alaska. Bottom: Paper clips are paramagnetic. This means that they exhibit induced magnetism when brought into contact with a permanent magnet.

CONTENTS

INTRODUCTION

Throughout history, people have witnessed electrical and magnetic phenomena. For many centuries, however, these phenomena were not understood. Ancient people observed the glowing auroras near the North and South poles of Earth, but they had no idea what caused these mysterious lights. It is now known that the auroras are caused by electrically charged particles being drawn into Earth's atmosphere, but ancient people had no scientific way to explain the lights. They could only imagine that supernatural forces, such as gods or the spirits of dead relatives, produced the lights.

Magnetism was another great mystery to our ancestors. The ancient Greeks noted the mysterious attractive powers of magnetite. Magnetite is a naturally magnetic mineral that was mined in a region of ancient Greece called Magnesia. The Greeks witnessed that magnetite attracted heavy materials

The glowing lights of the auroras are caused by particles from space being drawn into Earth's magnetic field. The charged particles excite atoms in the atmosphere, which cause them to glow.

such as iron. They were fascinated by this attraction, but they had no scientific way of understanding what force caused iron to be drawn to magnetite. Instead, they resorted to superstitious explanations, some believing that the magnetite had magical powers or that it possessed a soul.

The ancient Greeks were also fascinated with amber. Amber is fossilized tree resin. They noted that amber, when rubbed vigorously, tends to attract light objects such as hair and feathers. The Greeks did not understand this attraction that today is known as static electricity.

Although in the past people did not fully understand what caused electric and magnetic forces, it did not keep them from putting these forces to good use. The first magnetic compass was designed in China more than two thousand years ago. In time, the compass evolved into the invaluable magnetic needle compass that came to be used by sailors all over the world. Before the compass, sailors could only rely on the stars to determine direction. This worked on clear nights, but not when skies were cloudy or in the daytime. The magnetic compass, which always points to Earth's northern magnetic pole, allowed sailors to reliably determine direction throughout their journeys.

It was not until the seventeenth and eighteenth centuries that scientists first began to unravel the mysteries of electricity and magnetism by conducting experiments in controlled environments. They discovered that electric and magnetic phenomena are a result of positive and negative charges interacting with each other. By the late nineteenth century, atomic research finally began to reveal to scientists the previously mysterious nature of these positive and negative charges.

Researchers were able to isolate the negatively charged electron and, based on this discovery, the modern theory of the atom began to take shape.

Over the course of this research, the natural connection between electricity and magnetism was slowly revealed. It is this connection that forms the foundation of our current concept of the electromagnetic force. The electromagnetic force is one of the four known fundamental forces in nature. Without the presence of this force, the universe as we know it would not exist.

WHAT IS ELECTRICITY?

Electricity and magnetism are closely related. In fact, they are actually two aspects of the same force. This force is the electromagnetic force. The relationship between electricity and magnetism will be explored in detail in chapter 3. But first, what is electricity and how does it work?

POSITIVE AND NEGATIVE CHARGES

Electricity is a fundamental form of energy. It is the result of charges interacting with each other. There are two types of charges that are found in all matter. We call these two charges positive and negative. Every material and object in the universe contains both positive and negative charges. These charges are found in the atoms that make up all of the objects and materials in the universe.

The most important thing to remember about positive and negative charges is that like charges repel each other and unlike charges attract each other. Therefore, two positive charges will repel each other, while a positive and a negative charge will attract each other. It is this repulsion and attraction of charges that creates electricity. What we consider electricity is really the motion of charge.

ELECTRONS

To better understand how positive and negative charges inter-act with each other, we first need to understand the basic structure of an atom. An atom is composed of a central nucleus surrounded by electrons. The nucleus is composed of positively charged protons as well as neutrally charged neutrons. The nucleus has an overall

This traditional drawing of an atom illustrates electrons orbiting around a central nucleus. While not precisely what an atom looks like, it is a useful model for understanding an atom's basic structure.

positive charge. Surrounding the nucleus is an area of negatively charged electrons.

Different materials in the universe are made up of different types of atoms. These different atoms have varying numbers of protons, neutrons, and electrons. The number of protons and electrons in an atom is always balanced. Another difference in the types of atoms is that the nuclei of some atoms tend to hang onto their electrons more strongly than the nuclei of other atoms. This means that when you put different materials together, the material with the stronger-attracting nuclei can steal electrons from the material with the weaker-attracting nuclei. Thus, electrons will jump from one material to another.

This jumping of electrons can be observed by performing a simple experiment with an inflated balloon. If a person quickly rubs an inflated balloon back and forth across his or her hair and then slowly pulls it away, the person will notice that his or her hair is drawn up through the air toward the balloon. What exactly is happening here?

STATIC ELECTRICITY

It is important to remember that all of the materials in the world are made up of positive and negative charges and that unlike charges are attracted to each other. Since positive and negative charges are strongly attracted to each other, most things in the world carry an overall neutral charge. This is because something with an excess of positive charges attracts negative charges until the charges are equal.

When two materials are rubbed together, such as a balloon and a person's hair, it is possible for the charges to move from

This girl touches a static electricity generator and receives a large static electric charge. Since each strand of hair is getting the same charge, and like charges repel, her hairs push away from each other.

one material to another. When a balloon is rubbed against human hair, the atoms in the balloon take electrons from the atoms in the hair. Thus, the balloon now has an overall negative charge, and the hair is left with an overall positive charge. Since unlike charges attract, the person's hair and the balloon are now attracted to each other. The reason the electrons jump to the balloon instead of to the person's hair is because rubber is a material made up of atoms that tend to take electrons more strongly than the atoms that make up human hair.

It should be noted here that the atoms in all materials are actually part of larger structures called molecules. In reality, it is the molecules of the balloon that take electrons from the molecules of a person's hair. Regardless of this fact, the simpler atom model can be used to explain electrical phenomena. This is because the process of taking electrons is the same for individual atoms as it is for more complex molecules.

The rubbing of a person's hair against a balloon and the resulting attraction between the two materials is an example of static electricity. When performing this experiment, a person will notice that as the balloon is pulled farther away from his or her hair, the attraction between the charged materials is weakened. This is because electric forces get stronger as two objects get closer together and get weaker as they grow farther apart.

INDUCED CHARGE

In addition to the attraction between materials with unlike charges, there is an attraction between a negatively charged material and a neutrally charged material. Performing another experiment—this time with a negatively charged balloon and a neutrally charged piece of paper—will clearly demonstrate this attraction.

If a piece of paper is torn into tiny pieces and laid on a table, it can be seen that the small pieces are attracted to a negatively charged balloon. A rubbed balloon brought close to—but not touching—the bits of torn paper will draw the bits toward it. Unlike the human hair in the previous experiment, the paper itself is not positively charged. Why are the pieces of paper attracted to the balloon? This attraction is an example of induced charge.

When the negatively charged balloon is brought close to the bits of paper, the negative electrons in the paper's atoms are pushed away from the balloon. This is because like charges repel. At this point, the positively charged nuclei are closer to the balloon than the negatively charged electrons. This creates an attraction between the balloon and the paper.

At this point, the balloon, which has a negative charge, has induced a positive charge in the paper. We say that the paper has an induced charge because the paper itself has a net neutral charge and the balloon induces the paper to behave as if it has a positive charge.

ELECTRIC FIELDS

It can be seen that charged objects exert a force on each other. Based on this observation, a scientific model has been created that illustrates what is happening between two charged objects. This model is the concept of something called an electric field.

An electric field is illustrated with lines that radiate from a charged object. These lines point from positive to negative, and they never cross each other. The electric field model dictates that another charged object "feels" the force of a charged object and reacts to it.

CURRENT ELECTRICITY

In addition to static electricity, there is current electricity. Current electricity is a stream of continuously flowing electric charges. In order for electric charges to flow, they need an electromotive force. An electromotive force is a force that "pushes" charges. A common household battery generates voltage, which is an example of an electromotive force. Charges also need a conductor through which to move. A conductor is a material that will carry an electrical current. Copper wire is a common conductor.

An electromotive force connected to a conductor will cause electrons to move through the conductor and thus create an electric current. The electromotive force (in this case, the battery) and the conductor (the wire) together are called a circuit. A circuit becomes useful when it powers something that we need to work, such as a lightbulb or a motor.

TYPES OF ELECTRICAL CURRENT

There are two types of electrical current that we commonly use. One type of electrical current is called direct current. The other is called alternating current.

Shocking Machines

By the late seventeenth century, static electricity machines were appearing all across the continent of Europe. Through the use of a hand crank, these machines could generate large static charges. Just like rubbed amber, these static electricity machines held their charge until it was released. A charged machine could deliver miniature lightning bolts to metal rods that were brought close. It could also give a painful shock to a person who touched it.

Static electricity machines were used in carnivals to impress local audiences. The tiny bolts of lightning generated by these machines endlessly amazed people. Scientists at the time, however, considered electricity to be nothing more than a parlor trick. They could see no serious practical applications for the static charges.

It was not until 1729, when Stephen Gray of England demonstrated the principles of electrical conduction, that electricity first came to be seen as something useful. Current electricity, unlike static electricity, had great potential for practical application. In fact, by the late nineteenth century, current electricity was changing the way that people lived.

DIRECT CURRENT

Direct current is the simplest type of electrical current to understand. Direct current is the kind of current produced by batteries. It always travels in the same direction through the conductor.

If a wire is attached to both ends of a battery, a stream of electrons—the current—will flow from the negative terminal of the battery to the positive terminal of the battery. Since the current only flows in one direction, it is called direct current.

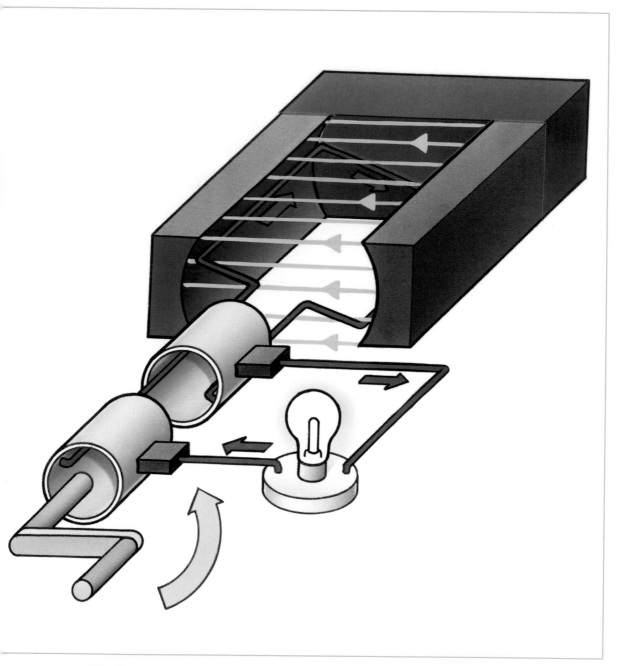

This diagram is of a simple alternate current generator, or alternator. It illustrates how a coil of wire spinning in the magnetic field of a permanent magnet creates a current through the wires and lightbulb that continually changes direction.

ALTERNATING CURRENT

Alternating current is the kind of current used to power homes, offices, and schools. It is the current provided by the electrical sockets in the walls of buildings. Alternating current is produced at a power plant. It is used because it is much easier to send over long distances than direct current.

Alternating current is produced when a coil of wire is spun in a magnetic field. Spinning a coil of wire in a magnetic field causes the electrons in the wire to move and therefore generate an electric current. The alternating current that is generated first travels in one direction and then in the opposite direction. The current alternates direction very rapidly—120 times per second in the United States.

CONDUCTORS

The reason that some metals are good conductors of electricity has to do with their atomic structure. The electrons in certain metal atoms, such as those found in copper, are not tied to their nuclei. Therefore, in a metal such as copper, electrons are free to move independently of their nuclei.

Electrons in metal move differently than electrons in non-conductive materials such as paper. When a negatively charged object, such as a balloon, is brought near paper, the balloon pushes the electrons of the paper atoms away. The electrons can't move very far though, as they are tied to the nuclei of their atoms. In a metal, the electrons are not tied to nuclei. They can, and do, move freely when the charged balloon is brought close.

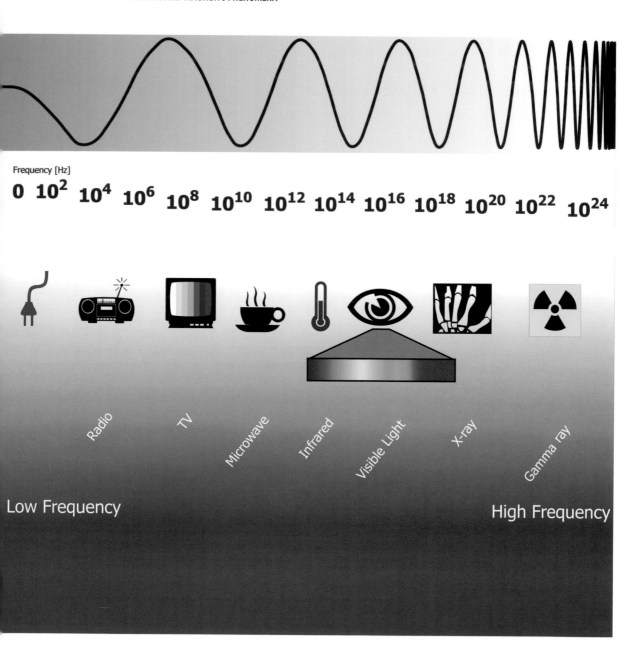

Frequency [Hz]

0 10² 10⁴ 10⁶ 10⁸ 10¹⁰ 10¹² 10¹⁴ 10¹⁶ 10¹⁸ 10²⁰ 10²² 10²⁴

Radio   TV   Microwave   Infrared   Visible Light   X-ray   Gamma ray

Low Frequency   High Frequency

The electromagnetic waves created by electrons in a circuit are part of the electromagnetic spectrum. The wavelengths of different types of electromagnetic radiation differ. On the left, with the longest wavelengths, are radio waves and microwaves. On the right, with the shortest, are X-rays and gamma rays. Shorter wavelengths contain more energy than longer wavelengths.

CIRCUITS

When a metal wire is attached to both ends of a battery, electrons are pushed through the wire and an electric current is generated. The electrons coming from the negative terminal of the battery push the electrons in the end of the wire. These pushed electrons do not move all the way through the wire, but rather act in relay. The electrons jump from one atom to another. As they jump, they bump the next electron along in a chain reaction called an electromagnetic wave. The electrons themselves don't travel very fast, but the electromagnetic wave that they create travels at nearly the speed of light.

2

WHAT IS MAGNETISM?

We have all seen a magnet. There are the types of magnets that we use to stick papers to our refrigerators, and there are bar magnets that you may have used in science class. We know that magnets can do certain things, but what exactly is a magnet?

THE NATURE OF A MAGNET

A magnet is a material or an object that produces a magnetic field. A magnetic field is the force that pulls on other materials, such as iron, and attracts and repels other magnets. We can't actually see a magnetic field, but we can prove that it exists in a number of ways.

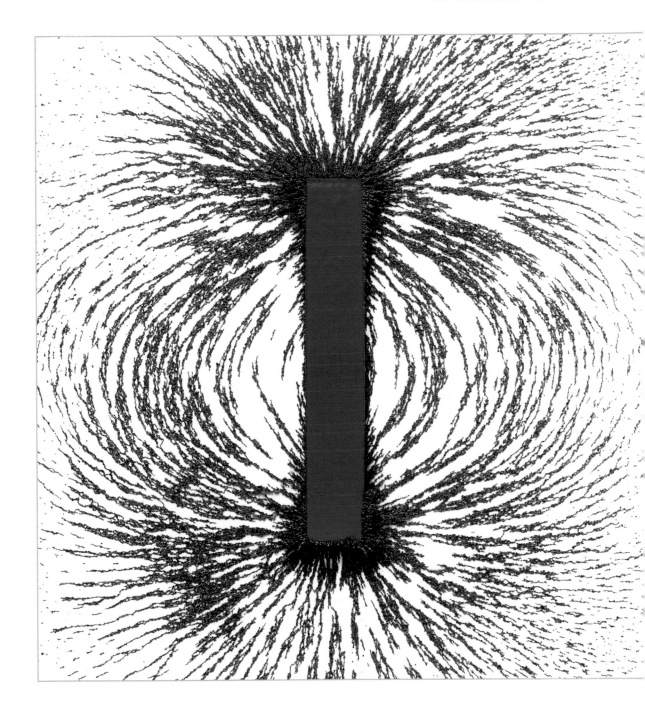

Iron filings, which are ferromagnetic, will line up along the magnetic field generated by a bar magnet.

A magnet is a dipole. This means that it always has two oppositely charged poles. We call these the north pole of the magnet and the south pole of the magnet. If you bring the like poles of two bar magnets together—north to north or south to south—you will notice that the poles repel, or resist, each other. The opposite is true if you bring unlike poles together. Unlike poles, north to south, attract each other.

A magnetic field is invisible to the naked eye. But to observe magnetic fields, let's look at how two magnets interact. If a compass is moved around the edges of a bar magnet, the compass needle will move in different directions. The needle of a compass is a magnet. Therefore, it lines up along the magnetic field lines of the bar magnet.

INDUCED MAGNETISM

In addition to attracting and repelling other magnets, magnets attract certain metals such as iron and nickel. Iron and nickel are ferromagnetic elements, which means that they are easily magnetized and tend to stay magnetized. When magnets interact with materials that are themselves nonmagnetic, it is called induced magnetism. Let's look at an example of induced magnetism.

If a bar magnet is placed under a piece of paper and iron filings are sprinkled on top of the paper and the paper is tapped lightly, a pattern will emerge. What is happening is that the ferromagnetic iron filings are lining up with the magnetic field produced by the bar magnet. The iron filings themselves are not magnetic, but when placed near a magnet, they act like magnets by lining up with the magnetic field.

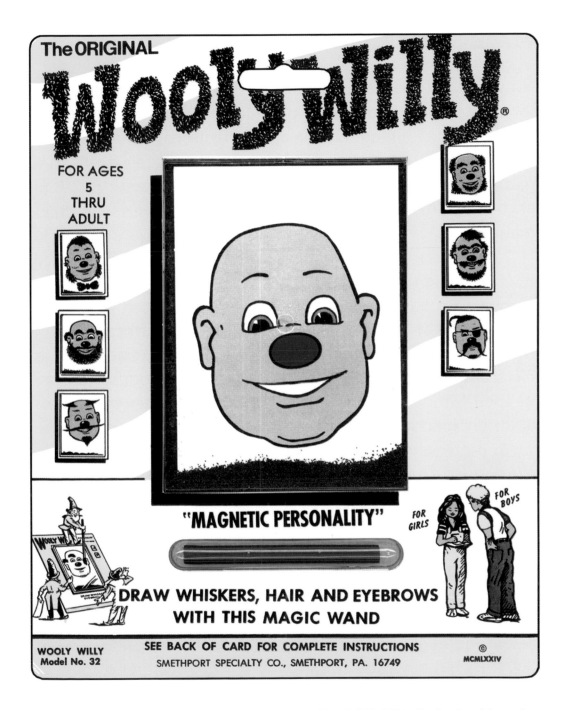

This children's toy uses a magnet and iron filings to add metal "hair" to the head and face of the character Wooly Willy. The "magic wand" used to move the iron filings is, in fact, a magnet.

MAGNETIC FIELDS

Now that we know how a magnetic field behaves, let's take a look at how a magnetic field comes to exist. In order for a material to produce a magnetic field, the electrons in that material must be lined up in a certain way. When the electrons in a material are lined up in such a way that the magnetic forces of each atom do not cancel each other out, that material becomes magnetic.

To understand how a material's electrons have to be aligned to create magnetism, we have to get down to the atomic level. You have probably seen atoms depicted with a positive nucleus (the protons and neutrons) surrounded by electrons orbiting the nucleus. This isn't exactly what is happening in an atom, as electrons do not actually orbit nuclei. But it is a model that can be used without exploring the much more complex theories of quantum mechanics.

To better understand magnetism, let's look back to electric currents for a moment. As discussed in chapter 1, an electric current is charged objects that are moving. Now consider the fact that an electric current moving in a circle acts just like a magnet. Therefore, if electrons are moving in circles around a nucleus, it can be understood that each atom itself acts as a tiny magnet, with a south magnetic pole and a north magnetic pole.

Since all materials are in fact made up of atoms (tiny magnets), one might expect all materials to be magnetic. This is not the case, however. For a material to be magnetic, most of the electrons in its atoms have to be orbiting in the same way (either clockwise or counterclockwise) and must be aligned in the same direction.

Geomagnetic Reversal

Of all the magnets that exist in the world, the biggest magnet of all is Earth itself. It may seem odd to think of a planet as being a magnet, but that is just what Earth is. Earth is magnetic because its hot liquid outercore contains molten iron. As the molten iron moves, it creates an electric current. In turn, this electric current creates a magnetic field around the planet.

If you find it strange that Earth is a magnet, you will probably find it even stranger that sometimes the North Pole of the planet is actually the South Pole. It's true. From time to time, about every 250,000 years, the magnetic poles of Earth actually switch. This means that the North Pole and the South Pole trade places. This is called geomagnetic reversal. Imagine looking at your compass and seeing the needle pointing south instead of north!

Nobody can say with any certainty what effect geomagnetic reversal would have on us if it happened today. This is because a geomagnetic reversal has never been witnessed by anyone who could have left a record of the event. The last reversal happened more than seven hundred thousand years ago. Since we are overdue for such an occurrence, however, it is possible that we will find out the effects of a geomagnetic reversal in the not-too-distant future.

MAGNETICS AND NONMAGNETICS

In most materials, the tiny atom-magnets are randomly oriented. This means that the effects of the separate little magnets cancel each other out. A magnet cannot be created by a group of randomly oriented magnets. Therefore, materials with randomly oriented atomic dipoles are nonmagnetic by nature.

If the electrons of the atoms in a particular material, such as iron, are free to line up together, that material can be magnetic. If they aren't, the material will be nonmagnetic. Now we can begin to visualize how the atoms are aligned in a permanent magnet.

How a Magnet Is Made

To understand how a permanent magnet is created, observe what happens when an existing permanent magnet comes near a paramagnetic material such as a paper clip. A paramagnetic material is a material in which there are not an equal number of aligned and anti-aligned electrons in each atom. Electrons tend to line up with an electric field, but other electrons aligning in the opposite direction cancel out most of them. Before the paper clip is brought close to the permanent magnet, the electrons in the clip are organized in random directions. As you bring the permanent magnet near the paper clip, the electrons in the paper clip line up with the magnetic field of the magnet. The paper clip itself now acts like a magnet, and it is attracted to the permanent magnet. At this point, the paper clip exhibits induced magnetism. When the permanent magnet is taken away, the electrons in

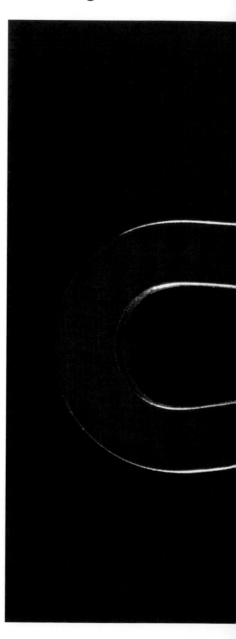

Paper clips, when brought into contact with a permanent magnet, will themselves display magnetic qualities. Here, two paperclips exhibit induced magnetism.

the paper clip return to a random orientation. Thus, the paper clip is left nonmagnetic.

Ferromagnetic materials, unlike paramagnetic materials, tend to stay magnetized. The same experiment, if performed

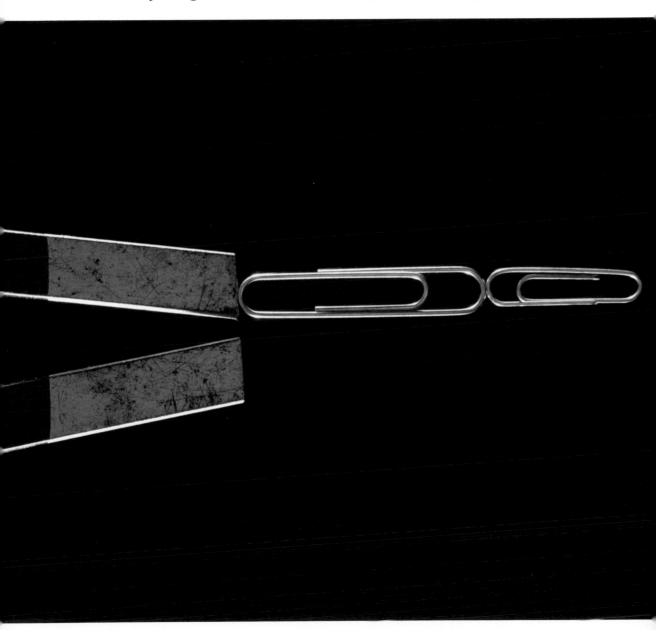

with a ferromagnetic material such as an iron nail, would have left the nail slightly magnetized, even after the permanent magnet was taken away.

In order to create a new, although weak, magnet, the nail can be rubbed along a bar magnet in the same direction and along the same pole. The nail must be rubbed multiple times across the magnet in order to become magnetized.

A permanent magnet can be destroyed as well as created. The easiest way to destroy a magnet is to smash it a few times on a hard surface. This will shake up the alignment of the atom's magnetic dipoles and disturb its magnetic field.

CHAPTER

3

THE CONNECTION BETWEEN ELECTRICITY AND MAGNETISM

Now that electricity and magnetism have been discussed, it is time to see how the two are related. Magnetism is in fact nothing more than electric currents. In other words, electricity and magnetism are actually the same thing.

CREATING AN ELECTROMAGNET

A simple experiment will demonstrate that magnetism is simply electric charges in motion. This experiment is easy to set up. It involves a D cell battery, two lengths of copper wire, an iron nail, a paper clip, and tape.

Before the experiment is set up, it will be observed that the nail itself is nonmagnetic. If the nail is held next to the paper clip, there is no attraction between the two objects. The experiment can now be set up in the following manner:

- Strip the plastic casing off each end of the copper wire.
- Coil the middle section of the wire neatly around the length of the nail.
- Tape the ends of the copper wire to each end of the battery.

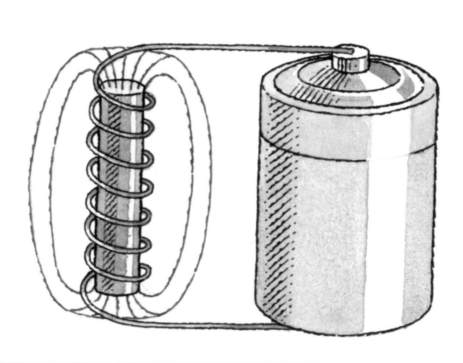

This is an example of an electromagnet created using a battery, some wire, and an iron rod. The red lines illustrate the magnetic field generated by the electromagnet.

If the experiment is set up correctly, the nail will now attract the paper clip. In other words, the nail will become a magnet. The magnet that is created with the battery, wire, and nail is called an electromagnet. The electric current running through the coiled wire has in fact created a magnetic field—the same exact magnetic field that is created by a permanent magnet.

How did the electric current in the wire turn the nail into a magnet? Remember that a circular electric current is itself a magnet. Just as an atom is a tiny magnet, with its orbiting electron, so is a coil of wire carrying an electric current.

When the nail is placed inside the electrified coil, the electrons in the nail "feel" the magnetic field generated by the coil of wire and line up with it. By lining up with the coil's magnetic field, the atoms of the nail will then create an even stronger magnetic field than the field generated by the coil alone.

If the nail is removed from the coil, it is still slightly magnetic. This is because iron is a ferromagnetic material. The atoms in the iron tend to stay lined up, even after the coil is removed. Thus, it is seen that a magnet can be created using an electric field, just as it can be created with a permanent magnet.

ELECTRIC CURRENTS AND MAGNETIC FIELDS

Because electric currents generate magnetic fields, they exert forces on other electric currents. Two current-carrying wires running parallel to each other will either attract or repel each other. If the currents of the wires are moving in opposite directions, the wires will attract each other. If the currents of the wires are moving in the same direction, the wires will repel

Hans Christian Oersted demonstrates that an electric current generates a magnetic field. Oerstead's nineteenth century discoveries helped spark the development of electromagnetic theory.

each other. This attraction and repulsion is caused by the magnetic fields generated by the moving current in the wires.

In 1820, Danish physicist Hans Christian Oersted demonstrated that electric currents generate magnetic fields. The magnetic field generated by an electric current flows in a circular direction around the current. Therefore, two current-carrying wires placed next to each other are influenced by each other's magnetic fields.

MAGNETIC FIELDS EXERT A FORCE ON MOVING CHARGES

It has been observed that electric currents exert a force on other electric currents. Now consider the fact that a magnet will exert a force on a moving electric charge. Picture a stream of electrons being shot from a gun into a window. The stream moves in a straight line into the window. Now if a magnet is placed on the opposite side of the window in the spot that the electrons are hitting, the stream of electrons will be deflected away from that spot. This is because the magnet is in fact nothing but a collection of tiny electric currents. These currents exert a force on the stream of electrons in the same manner that two current-carrying wires exert a force on each other.

A CHANGING MAGNETIC FIELD GENERATES AN ELECTRIC FIELD

We have established that a magnet has an associated magnetic field. Now consider what happens when a magnet is moved. If a magnet is moved, stationary objects positioned next to the magnet will feel the relative strength of the magnetic field change as the magnet moves. This shows that a changing magnetic field generates an electric field.

The electric field generated by a changing magnetic field can be explained with a simple demonstration using a toilet paper roll, a copper wire, a compass, and a magnet. The copper wire is first coiled around the toilet paper roll, with the coils all wrapped in the same direction. Then the wire is coiled around the compass, again with the coils all wrapped in the same direction. The wire is then joined together at each end to complete the circuit.

If a magnet is moved in and out of the tube, the needle of the compass will move slightly each time the magnet moves. The movement of the needle is caused by the electric field generated by the moving magnet. In turn, it is also true that a changing electric field generates a magnetic field. This was seen in the magnetic field generated by the current-carrying wires.

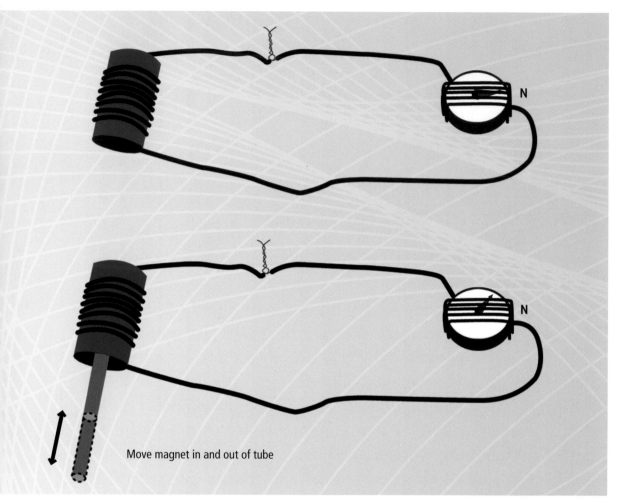

Move magnet in and out of tube

This experiment illustrates how a changing magnetic field generates an electric field. Notice that the needle jumps slightly when the magnet is moved in and out of the tube. The movement of the needle is caused by the magnetic field generated by the electric current flowing through the wire.

These two facts are important, as they are the principle upon which electric generators function. The electricity used to power buildings and streetlights is produced in generators where a coil of wire spins in a magnetic field. The movement of the coil generates a steady stream of electrons.

Monopoles vs. Dipoles

Although electricity and magnetism are both aspects of the electromagnetic force, there is one notable difference between electric charges and a magnet. Electric charges can exist as dipoles as well as monopoles. Magnets, however, can only exist as dipoles.

For example, if a negatively charged object, like a rubbed balloon, is brought near a neutral object, such as a piece of paper, the atoms in the neutral object will behave as dipoles. That is, the negatively charged object will push the electrons away from it and pull the positive charges toward it. But an electric charge can also exist as a monopole. This is to say that positive and negative charges can be isolated. When electrons jump from one atom to another, the electrons exist as monopoles.

Unlike electric charges, magnets can never exist as monopoles. If a magnet is chopped in half, it will still exist as a dipole. Even if it is chopped into consecutively smaller pieces all the way down to the atomic level, it will remain a dipole. The reason is simple: An atom is itself a tiny magnet. Furthermore, even if an atom is broken apart, a magnetic monopole cannot be found. Simply put, a magnet must always exist as a dipole, having both a north magnetic pole and a south magnetic pole.

ELECTROMAGNETIC WAVES

Light waves are a type of electromagnetic wave. The light waves that illuminate our universe are in fact composed of oscillating magnetic and electric fields. Since changing magnetic fields generate electric fields, and changing electric fields generate magnetic fields, light waves are able to move continuously through the universe. They are indeed self-powered.

THE HISTORY OF ELECTRICAL AND MAGNETIC DISCOVERIES

Research of magnetic and electrical phenomena did not begin in earnest until the seventeenth century. A British physician named William Gilbert was the scientific pioneer who would get the ball rolling in these fields of study. His discoveries paved the way for later research into electricity and magnetism.

In Gilbert's day, very little was understood about electricity and magnetism. He created unique inventions so that he could better study these phenomena. By performing experiments using these inventions, Gilbert was able to come to a new understanding of how magnetism and electricity work.

WILLIAM GILBERT'S GENIUS

One of William Gilbert's inventions was a spherical magnet constructed out of magnetite. Gilbert called his Earth-shaped magnet terella, which means "little Earth." He performed a series of experiments using a magnetic compass in conjunction with the terella. He observed that the compass needle always lined up with the terella's north and south poles, just as it does with the magnetic poles of Earth. He also noticed that the compass needle tilted down toward the sphere as he moved the compass toward the North Pole. Based on the results of his experiments, Gilbert was able to conclude that Earth in fact is a giant magnet.

Gilbert created another invention, which he called the versorium. Versorium means "turn about" in Latin. Gilbert's versorium consisted of an iron needle rotating on a sharp point. He magnetized the needle for some experiments and left it unmagnetized for others. Using his versorium, he made the important discovery that the force of a magnet became stronger as it approached the versorium's needle. Gilbert had unknowingly stumbled upon the inverse square law of magnetism, which is a concept that would not be fully understood until nearly two hundred years later.

In another set of experiments, Gilbert studied the attractive forces of charged amber. He placed rubbed amber near a non-magnetized needle in his versorium. He noticed that the needle responded to the static charge on the amber. He experimented with other charged materials like glass and wax and noticed that they, too, attracted the needle. Gilbert called materials

Magnetizing of iron, a page from William Gilbert's highly influential book *De Magnete*, is seen here.

such as amber "electrics" because they could be rubbed to produce a charge. He also noted that only objects containing iron could be turned into magnets.

In 1600, Gilbert published the results of his experiments in a book called *De Magnete, Magneticisque Corporibus, et de Magno Magnete Tellure* ("On the Magnet and Magnetic Bodies, and On That Great Magnet the Earth"). His book is among the most important scientific works published during the Scientific Revolution of the sixteenth and seventeenth centuries. Gilbert's discoveries led to a revolution in scientific research.

FROM STATIC ELECTRICITY TO CURRENT ELECTRICITY

In 1729, another Englishman, retired cloth dyer Stephen Gray, performed some experiments that laid the groundwork for the development of current electricity. Unlike static electricity, which was little more than a sideshow attraction, current electricity had enormous potential for practical application. Using a wire suspended with silk thread, Gray was able to send an electric current though the wire.

Based on his experiments, Gray determined that there were two classes of materials. The first class, called conductors, was capable of carrying electricity. The second class, called insulators, was not.

Although Gray had successfully created a brief electric current, it would be decades before current electricity could be used for everyday applications. The reason for this was the lack of a continuous source of electrical power to create a steady electrical current. Such a power source was not to exist until sixty years later, when Alessandro Volta created the first voltaic battery.

UNRAVELING THE MYSTERIES OF ELECTRICITY

In the early eighteenth century, scientists were struggling to understand the nature of electric charges. In 1733 and 1734, French chemist Charles François de Cisternay du Fay performed some key experiments that led him to construct a theory of electricity. Du Fay's theory can be called a two-fluid theory, as it imagined two different types of fluids present in objects that were responsible for electrical forces.

In his experiments, du Fay charged a leaf of gold using a friction generator. He noted that the charged leaf was repulsed by glass. He also noted that the leaf was attracted to charged wax and charged amber. To explain the attraction and repulsion, du Fay imagined two distinct fluids at work in the materials. He called the fluid that he imagined caused a charge on the glass "vitreous." Vitreous is Latin for "of glass." He called the fluid responsible for the charge in the amber "resinous." Du Fay reasoned that materials with an excess of the same fluid repelled one another and those with an excess of different fluids attracted each other. He imagined that the gold leaf and the glass both had an excess of vitreous fluid and that they therefore repelled each other.

Du Fay was on to something important, but he was unable to accurately determine the true nature of electricity. It would take a thinker across the Atlantic Ocean to progress beyond the two-fluid theory and develop a more accurate theory of how electricity worked. This person was Benjamin Franklin.

BENJAMIN FRANKLIN

Benjamin Franklin imagined that electricity was a stream of some sort of charged particles. Unlike du Fay, however, Franklin reasoned that the movement of just one type of particle could explain all electrical phenomena. Du Fay's two-fluid theory had failed to accurately explain certain electrical phenomena. Franklin's theory, on the other hand, was comprehensive. He

This print shows Benjamin Franklin and his son William flying a kite during an electrical storm. In 1752, Franklin published a paper describing how he conducted lightning with a kite.

presented the idea that when an object is rubbed, it either gains charges or gives up charges.

Franklin understood that conductors, such as metal wire, allow electricity to move and that insulators do not. He also knew that the particles that made up electricity must be very small indeed. They must be, he reasoned, as there was no other way that they could move through dense metals such as metal wire. What Franklin was on to was nothing less than the concept of electron movement. Of course, since the atom had

Light Is a Particle and a Wave

In 1905, Albert Einstein published a revolutionary set of papers that completely changed how we understand the nature of light. Forty years earlier, a young Scottish physicist named James Clerk Maxwell had created a set of mathematical equations that described the nature of electromagnetic radiation. Maxwell's equations describe light as a wave of oscillating electrical and magnetic fields.

Einstein theorized that light, in addition to being an electromagnetic wave, is a collection of distinct particles of energy. He termed the particles "photons." He explained the existence of these photons by observing a phenomenon known as the photoelectric effect.

When electromagnetic waves, such as light, strike a piece of metal, they can knock free some of the electrons in the metal. Einstein reasoned that if light is merely a wave, increasing the intensity of the light would push the electrons that were knocked free with more energy. It turned out, however, that this did not happen. Instead, the light wave, when intensified, simply knocked more electrons free from the metal, and those extra electrons still had the same amount of energy. So increasing the intensity does not increase the strength of the light wave; it just increases the number of light particles being emitted.

not yet been discovered, Franklin was limited by the scientific knowledge of the day.

LINKING ELECTRICITY AND MAGNETISM

In 1785, French scientist Charles de Coulomb discovered an important relationship between electricity and magnetism. He revealed this relationship using a torsion balance, an instrument that he had designed himself.

Using the torsion balance, Coulomb discovered what is called the inverse square law for electrical force. The inverse square law for electrical force dictates that the force between two charged particles is directly proportional to the product of their charge and inversely (oppositely) proportional to the square of the distance between them. Coulomb later found that the inverse square law also applied to magnetic force. It seemed to Coulomb that magnetism and electricity must somehow be related if they follow the same law.

The link was soon to be confirmed with the help of a most important invention: the battery. The battery was an extremely useful invention because it offered an easy way to create a continuous current that could then be studied.

THE VOLTAIC BATTERY

In 1800, Italian physicist Alessandro Volta demonstrated the first battery. Volta's battery produced a different type of electricity than static electricity. The voltaic battery produced a continuous stream of electrical current. Voltaic batteries could be built to very large sizes, and they could produce immense amounts of power.

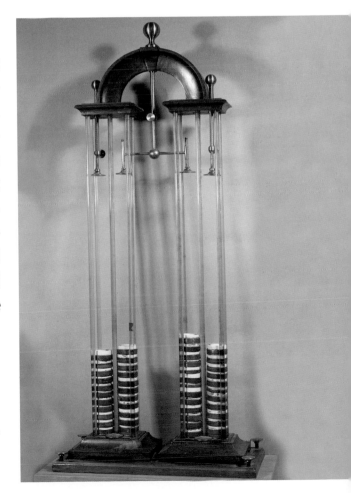

A voltaic battery, such as this one, was the first battery created. It is capable of producing a continuous current of electricity.

Volta's new electrical source opened up a world of electrical experiments to scientists. It also led to the creation of such practical and hugely significant electrical inventions as the telegraph. Within a few decades, the ability to create current electricity would change the face of the world.

OERSTED'S RIGHT-HAND RULE

In 1820, Hans Christian Oersted discovered an important link between electricity and magnetism. He set up an experiment using a wire, a battery, and a magnetic compass. He placed a wire above the compass. Then he connected the ends of the wire to a battery. This caused an electrical current to flow through the wire. Just as the current started to flow, Oersted noticed that the compass needle quickly moved perpendicularly to the electric current.

This discovery allowed Oersted to conclude that a magnetic circulation always flows around an electric current in a conductor. He also noted that this flow moved in a consistent direction. We can refer to Oersted's right-hand rule to determine the direction of magnetic circulation. If you are holding a wire in your right fist that is positioned vertically and the current is flowing upward, the magnetic field generated by the wire will flow in the direction that your fingers are pointing.

ELECTRODYNAMICS

In September 1820, a French professor of physics named André-Marie Ampère witnessed a demonstration of Oersted's electromagnetism. Ampère was fascinated by the demonstration, and shortly thereafter, he succeeded in drafting the fundamental laws for the field of electrodynamics. Electrodynamics is the theory of how electricity and magnets interact.

Ampère's mathematical contributions to science helped provide the world with a most practical invention—the electromagnet. Electromagnets are incredibly important in the modern world. Many things that we rely on every day, such as speakers, electric motors, and even particle accelerators, could not exist without the electromagnet.

PRACTICAL APPLICATIONS OF ELECTRICITY

The magnetic and electrical discoveries of the nineteenth century led to the creation of valuable technologies. The telegraph, for example, utilized the magnetic effects of electricity and allowed people to communicate over distances at a speed never before dreamed.

British chemist and physicist Michael Faraday created what was perhaps the most important electromagnetic invention. Because of his research, the first electric motor came to be in 1831. It would not be long before the electric motor changed the world.

Faraday's motor was simple in its construction. It consisted of a magnetic rod placed in a dish of mercury. A wire was dangled from above that magnet, down into the mercury. Faraday then created a circuit between a battery, the wire, and the mercury. The battery sent a current through the wire, which in turn created a magnetic field around the wire. The interaction between the stationary magnetic rod and the magnetic field of the wire caused the wire to rotate around the rod.

Michael Faraday, seen here, was a brilliant scientist credited with inventing the first electric motor. The electric motor is one of the single most important inventions ever created.

In addition to inventing the electric motor, Faraday answered a pressing question regarding electrodynamics. Could magnetism generate electricity, just as electricity generated magnetism? Faraday considered that if it took a moving current of electricity to produce magnetism, perhaps some movement of magnetism was required to generate electricity. Based on experiments using a moving magnetic field to generate electricity, Faraday was able to invent an induction generator. His generator converted mechanical energy into electricity. A mechanical force turned a wire coil in a magnetic field, causing electricity to flow in the wire.

THE WIRELESS AGE

In 1889, German physicist Heinrich Hertz produced the first radio wave. His discovery of radio waves marked the end of the telegraph and the dawn of the wireless age. People could now communicate with each other directly through the air.

Radio waves are a type of electromagnetic wave. There are many different types of electromagnetic waves. All of them together make up the electromagnetic spectrum. Light itself is an electromagnetic wave. It's in the part of the spectrum that we can actually see. Other waves, such as radio waves, X-rays, and gamma rays, are invisible to the naked eye.

DISSECTING THE ATOM

By the turn of the twentieth century, the power of electricity was changing the world. Ironically, physicists still had not discovered just what the mysterious particles that created electricity were. It would take a technological invention, the cathode-ray tube, to help scientists at last isolate these mysterious particles.

Cathode-ray tubes were the predecessors to the tubes used in televisions. They are glass vacuum tubes, meaning that the air has been pumped out of them. A platinum plate is placed at one end of the tube (the negative terminal) and a metal plate is placed at the other end (the positive terminal). When a current is run through the tube, a glowing stream of particles shoots out from the platinum plate to the metal plate.

These particular rays puzzled scientists at first. Unlike light and other electromagnetic waves, these rays could be deflected by a magnetic field. On the other hand, they could also pass straight though pieces of metal foil, which was a behavior that other particles did not share.

Finally, in 1897, a British physicist named J. J. Thomson solved the elusive mystery of just what electricity consisted of. Thomson determined that the rays in cathode tubes were actually a stream of electrons. He proved this by simultaneously subjecting the stream of electrons to both a magnetic field and an electric field. Using this method, he was able to calculate the mass of the particles. Thomson's discovery set the stage for our current model of atomic structure.

WHERE DO WE GO FROM HERE?

Over the course of the past century, the practical applications of the electromagnetic force have changed the way in which we live. The electric motor revolutionized the way that work is done. The power grid that provides electricity to our homes and workplaces has benefited us in more ways than we can count. So what are a few of the new electromagnetic innovations in the works that may someday change the world again?

WIRELESS ELECTRICITY

In the 1890s, wireless electricity was first experimented with by Nikola Tesla, an Austrian inventor and engineer. This form of electricity is being further developed today. While still in its early stages

Particle Accelerators

There are many uses for electromagnets. Electric motors, junkyard cranes, and even the earphones that plug into your MP3 player all make use of electromagnets. The most powerful electromagnets are used in a machine called a particle accelerator.

A particle accelerator is a huge circular tunnel that is used to smash together particles such as atoms and electrons. An accelerator uses electric fields to accelerate atomic and subatomic particles. Electromagnets keep the particles confined in a narrow beam. The largest particle accelerator is the **Large Hadron Collider**, which is seventeen miles (twenty-seven kilometers) in circumference.

Physicists use particle accelerators to study matter and energy. Smashing the nucleus of an atom allows scientists to study the even smaller parts that make up the atom's nucleus. Subatomic particles, such as quarks, can only be studied if an atom is first smashed. The Large Hadron Collider's beams were turned on for the first time on March 30, 2010.

Shown here is the magnet core of the Large Hadron Collider in Geneva, Switzerland. Particle accelerators use electromagnets to focus colliding streams of particles. This research helps scientists to better understand the nature of subatomic particles.

of development, this technology has already advanced to the stage where it is able to power a lightbulb from a few feet away. Wireless electricity could change the world of tomorrow, much as current electricity changed the world more than a century ago.

Wireless electricity works by a process called resonant energy transfer. This process involves two coils. One coil, which is called the power coil, is caused to resonate, which produces a magnetic field. The other coil, called the power capture coil, is placed at a distance from the power coil. The power capture coil picks up the magnetic field generated by the power coil and then converts the magnetic field back into electricity.

ELECTROMAGNETIC TRANSPORTATION

Electromagnetic technology could soon change the way that people travel. Currently, there is no alternative to airplane travel if people need to go long distances in a short period of time. But a new type of train, which is powered by the use of electromagnets, may soon offer an alternative. This train is called a maglev train, named after magnetic levitation, and it is already in use in the Chinese city of Shanghai.

A maglev train is unlike a traditional train. It does not have wheels or a conventional engine. Instead of fossil fuels, it is propelled by a magnetic field. A maglev train is capable of traveling at speeds of more than 300 miles (483 km) per hour.

Considering that airports are usually built far from city centers and the frequent delays that people must deal with during airline travel, maglev trains could save travelers a great deal of time. In addition to reducing travel time, the use of a magnetic

The Shanghai maglev train is the first commercial magnetic levitation train in the world. It takes passengers to and from Shanghai International Airport.

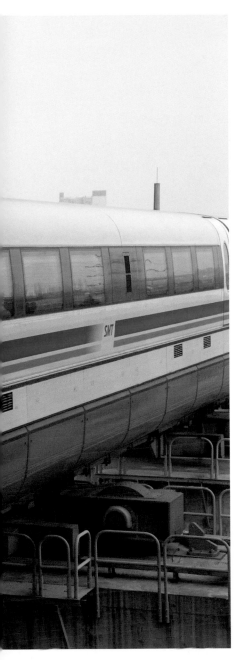

field to power high-speed transportation has the added benefit of being environmentally friendly. Airplanes burn large amounts of fossil fuels, which are bad for the environment.

Another technology that is being developed is the electromagnetic wheel. A car equipped with electromagnetic wheels is not powered by a traditional engine and drive train, but by the wheels themselves. Electromagnetic wheels consist of two magnets. One is an electromagnet, and the other is a permanent magnet. The electromagnet is powered by a battery, and it is of the same polarity as the permanent magnet. The repulsive force between the two magnets is converted into motion.

The maglev train and the electromagnetic wheel are just two cutting-edge examples of electromagnetic technology. The practical applications of electromagnetism are endless. They are limited only by the imaginations of the scientists, engineers, and entrepreneurs who can develop these technologies to help us live better in the years to come.

GLOSSARY

alternating current An electric current that
reverses its direction at regular intervals.

aurora Broad bands of light that have a magnetic
and electrical source and appear in the night sky
in the polar regions of Earth.

battery An electric cell that stores a charge and
provides a voltage.

circuit The complete path of an electric current.

compass A navigational device used for determin-
ing direction by means of a magnetic needle.

conductor A substance or body that can allow electricity to pass through it.

current electricity The name given to charges
in motion.

dipole Magnetized poles that are equal and oppositely charged and separated by some distance.

direct current An electric current flowing in only
one direction.

electricity A form of energy that is found in nature
but can also be produced by friction, by the action
of chemicals, or by means of a generator.

electromagnet A core of magnetic material surrounded by a coil of wire through which an
electric current is passed to magnetize the core.

electromagnetic force A force that affects
charged particles; one of the four known fundamental forces in nature.

electromagnetic wave A wave, such as a radio wave or a wave of visible light, that consists of an associated electric and magnetic effect and travels at the speed of light.

electromotive force The work per unit charge required to carry a positive charge around a closed circuit in an electric field.

electron A subatomic particle that carries a negative charge of electricity and travels around the nucleus of an atom.

ferromagnetic Of or relating to substances, such as iron and nickel, that are easily magnetized.

induced charge A separation of charges in a neutral object that causes the object to act like a charged object.

insulator A material that is a poor conductor of electricity.

magnetism The property of attracting certain metals or producing a magnetic field as shown by a magnet or a conductor carrying an electric current.

magnetite A black mineral that is an oxide of iron and is strongly attracted by a magnet.

neutron An uncharged subatomic particle that occurs in the nucleus of an atom and has a mass slightly greater than that of the proton.

nucleus The central part of an atom that consists of protons and neutrons.

paramagnetic Describing a material that is weakly attracted by the poles of a magnet but does not retain magnetism.

proton A subatomic particle that occurs in the nucleus of an atom and carries a positive charge equal in size to the negative charge of an electron.

static electricity Isolated stationary charges.

FOR MORE INFORMATION

American Museum of Science and Energy

300 S. Tulane Avenue

Oak Ridge, TN 37830

(865) 576-3200

Web site: http://www.amse.org

The American Museum of Science and Energy is dedicated to the exploration of energy and basic science principles. Its Web site includes fun activities and is a great resource for report writing and information.

California Science Center

700 Exposition Park Drive

Los Angeles, CA 90037

(323) 724-3623

Web site: http://www.californiasciencecenter.org

The California Science Center offers fun and informative permanent exhibits presented in interactive worlds.

Children's Museum

950 Trout Brook Drive

West Hartford, CT 06119

(860) 231-2824

Web site: http://thechildrensmuseumct.org

The Children's Museum is a science museum

with a permanent science dome exhibit as well as a planetarium.

Children's Museum of Science and Technology
250 Jordan Road (in Rensselaer Technology Park)
Troy, NY 12180
(518) 235-2120
Web site: http://www.cmost.com
The mission of the Children's Museum of Science and Technology is to foster a sense of wonder and discovery in young minds.

Discovery Centre
1593 Barrington Street
Halifax, NS B3J 1Z7
Canada
(902) 492-4422
Web site: http://www.discoverycentre.ns.ca
The Discovery Centre presents science and technology in an entertaining environment. It provides live demonstrations, hands-on-experiments, and educational workshops.

Discovery Science Center
2500 North Main Street
Santa Ana, CA 92705
(714) 542-2823
Web site: http://www.discoverycube.org
The Discovery Science Center is a nonprofit organization dedicated to educating young minds through interactive exhibits and programs.

Ontario Science Center
770 Don Mills Road
Toronto, ON M3C 1T3
Canada
(888) 696-1110
Web site: http://www.ontariosciencecentre.ca
The Ontario Science Centre's mission is "to delight, inform,
    and challenge visitors through engaging and thought-pro-
    voking experiences in science and technology."

WEB SITES

Due to the changing nature of Internet links, Rosen Publishing
has developed an online list of Web sites related to the subject
of this book. This site is updated regularly. Please use this link
to access the list:

www.rosenlinks.com/sms/eamp

FOR FURTHER READING

Adamczyk, Peter, and Paul-Francis Law. *Electricity and Magnetism*. London, England: Usborne Publishing, 2008.

Cheshire, Gerard. *Electricity and Magnetism*. Mankato, MN: Black Rabbit Books, 2006.

Gardner, Robert. *Easy Genius Science Projects with Electricity and Magnetism*. Berkeley Heights, NJ: Enslow Publishers, 2009

Gray, Theodore. *The Elements: A Visual Exploration of Every Known Atom in the Universe*. New York, NY: Black Dog and Leventhal Publishers, 2009.

Jennings, Terry J. *Magnets*. Mankato, MN: Black Rabbit Books, 2009.

Murray, Julie. *Magnets*. Edina, MN: ABDO Publishing Company, 2007.

Rau, Dana. *Electricity and Magnetism*. Ann Arbor, MI: Cherry Lake Publishing, 2009.

Roxbee Cox, Phil. *Atoms and Molecules*. London, England: Usborne Publishing, 2008.

Schuh, Mari. *Magnetism*. Minneapolis, MN: Bellweather Media, 2008.

Sussman, Art. *Dr. Art's Guide to Science: Connecting Atoms, Galaxies, and Everything in Between*. Hoboken, NJ: Wiley, 2006.

Woodford, Chris. *Experiments with Electricity and Magnetism*. New York, NY: Gareth Stevens Publishing, 2010.

BIBLIOGRAPHY

Blakely, Sandra. *Myth, Ritual and Metallurgy in Ancient Greece and Recent Africa.* Cambridge, England: Cambridge University Press, 2006.

Bodanis, David. *Electric Universe: The Shocking True Story of Electricity.* New York, NY: Crown Publishing Group, 2005.

Bozorth, Richard M. *Ferromagnetism.* Hoboken, NJ: Wiley, 1993.

Christian von Baeyer, Hans. *Taming the Atom.* Mineola, NY: Dover Publications, 2000.

Cohen, I. Bernard. *Benjamin Franklin's Science.* Cambridge, MA: Harvard University Press, 1996.

Cohen-Tannoudji, Claude. *Atoms in Electromagnetic Fields.* Hackensack, NJ: World Scientific Publishing Company, 2004.

Dunlop, David J., Ozden Ozdemir, and David Edwards, ed. *Rock Magnetism: Fundamentals and Frontiers.* Cambridge, England: Cambridge University Press, 2001.

Gignoux, Damien, Michel Schelnker, and Etienne du Tremolet de Lacheisserie, ed. *Magnetism.* New York, NY: Springer-Verlag 2004.

Grigoryev, V., G. Myakishev, and George Yankovsky, trans. *Forces of Nature.* Honolulu, HI: University Press of the Pacific, 2001.

Hofmann, James R. *Andre-Marie Ampère: Enlightenment and Electrodynamics*. Cambridge, England: Cambridge University Press, 2006.

Kovetz, Attay. *Electromagnetic Theory*. New York, NY: Oxford University Press, 2000.

Mazur, Glen A., and Peter A. Zurlis. *Electrical Principles and Practices*. Orland Park, IL: American Technical Publishers, 2007.

Robertson, William. *Electricity and Magnetism*. Arlington, VA: NSTA Press, 2005.

Schiffer, Michael Brian. *Draw the Lightning Down: Benjamin Franklin and Electrical Technology in the Age of Enlightenment*. Berkley, CA: University of California Press, 2006.

Sussman, Art. *Dr. Art's Guide to Science: Connecting Atoms, Galaxies, and Everything in Between*. Hoboken, NJ: Jossey-Bass, 2006.

U.S. Bureau of Naval Personnel. *Basic Electricity*. New York, NY: Dover Publications, 1979.

Valkenburg, Van. *Basic Electricity*. Florence, KY: Cengage Learning, 1995.

INDEX

M

maglev train, 51–53
magnetic compass, 6
magnetic field, 17, 20, 22, 24, 28, 31–35,
    42, 45, 47, 48, 51–53
magnetite, 5–6, 37
magnets
    how they are made, 26–28
    and nonmagnets, 25
    properties of, 20–22, 32–33
Maxwell, James Clerk, 42
molecules, 12
monopoles, 35

N

neutrons, 9–10, 13, 24
nickel, 22
nucleus, 9–10, 13, 17, 24, 50

O

Oersted, Hans Christian, 32, 44
Oersted's right-hand rule, 44

P

paramagnetic material, 26
particle accelerators, 50

R

radio waves, 47
resonant energy transfer, 51

S

static electricity, 6, 10–12, 39, 43
    machines, 15

T

telegraph, 44, 45, 47
terella, 37
Tesla, Nikola, 49
Thomson, J. J., 48
torsion balance, 42

V

vensorium, 37
Volta, Alessandro, 39, 43–44
voltaic battery, 39, 43–44

W

wireless electricity, 49, 51

photons, 42
photoelectric effect, 42
protons, 6–7, 8–14, 24

ABOUT THE AUTHOR

Dean Galiano is a writer who lives and works in New York City. Galiano has written a number of books about scientific phenomena, including a comprehensive four-book series about weather called the Weather Watcher's Library.

PHOTO CREDITS

Cover (top), pp. 1, 4–5, 9, 26–27, 54, 56, 61, 63 Shutterstock; cover (bottom) © www.istockphoto.com/Tommounsey; chapter art (top) © www.istockphoto. com/Sebastian Kaulitzki; chapter art (left) © www.istockphoto.com/DSGpro; pp. 11, 50 © AP Images; p. 16 © Dorling Kindersley; p. 18 Friedrich Saurer/Photo Researchers; p. 21 Cordelia Molloy/Photo Researchers; p. 23 © Courtesy Patch Products; p. 30 John Woodcock © Dorling Kindersley; pp. 32, 38 The Granger Collection; p. 41 Library of Congress Prints & Photographs Collection; p. 43 Scala/White Images/Art Resource, NY; p. 46 Hulton Archive/Getty Images; pp. 52-53 Gavin Hellier/Robert Harding World Imagery/Getty Images

Designer: Sam Zavieh; Editor: Karolena Bielecki;
Photo Researcher: Marty Levick

YAdult
QC
527.2
.G35
2011

Galiano, Dean.
    Electric and magnetic
phenomena.

GAYLORD